TOXIC
CREATURES

The Deathstalker
Scorpion

Laura L. Sullivan

Cavendish
Square

New York

Published in 2018 by Cavendish Square Publishing, LLC
243 5th Avenue, Suite 136, New York, NY 10016

First Edition

Website: cavendishsq.com

This publication represents the opinions and views of the author based on his or her personal experience, knowledge, and research. The information in this book serves as a general guide only. The author and publisher have used their best efforts in preparing this book and disclaim liability rising directly or indirectly from the use and application of this book.

CPSIA Compliance Information: Batch #CS17CSQ

All websites were available and accurate when this book was sent to press.

Library of Congress Cataloging-in-Publication Data

Names: Sullivan, Laura L.
Title: The deathstalker scorpion / Laura L. Sullivan.
Description: New York : Cavendish Square Publishing, 2018. | Series: Toxic creatures | Includes index.
Identifiers: ISBN 9781502625960 (pbk.) | ISBN 9781502625915 (library bound) |
ISBN 9781502625779 (6 pack) | ISBN 9781502625885 (ebook)
Subjects: LCSH: Leiurus quinquestriatus--Juvenile literature. | Scorpions--Juvenile literature.
Classification: LCC QL458.72.B8 S85 2018 | DDC 595.4'6--dc23

Editorial Director: David McNamara
Editor: Fletcher Doyle
Copy Editor: Nathan Heidelberger
Associate Art Director: Amy Greenan
Designer: Alan Sliwinski
Production Coordinator: Karol Szymczuk
Photo Research: J8 Media

The photographs in this book are used by permission and through the courtesy of: Cover Daniel Rosenberg; throughout book, Deliverance/Shutterstock.com; p. 4 Gregory MD/Science Source/Getty Images; p. 6 mapichai/Shutterstock.com; p. 7 megastocker/Shutterstock.com; p. 8 Anatolii Kokoza/Wikimedia Commons/File:L quinquestriatus2.jpg/CC BY-SA 3.0; p. 11 czorny01/iStock/Thinkstock; p. 13 Opka/Shutterstock.com; p. 14 LenSoMy/iStock/Thinkstock; p. 17 Danny S./Wikimedia Commons/File:Leiurus quinquestriatus Giftstachel.jpg/CC BY-SA 4.0; p. 18 Charlotte Roemer/Wikimedia Commons/File:Otonycteris hemprichii.jpg/CC BY-SA 3.0; p. 21 Science & Society Picture Library/Getty Images; p. 22, 26 Balint Porneczi/Bloomberg/Getty Images; p. 24 Wikimedia Commons/Blondis at English Wikipedia/File:MRI glioma 28 yr old male.JPG/Public Domain; p. 27 Ester Inbar/Wikimedia Commons/File:Deathstalker ST 07.jpg/CC BY-SA 3.0.

Printed in the United States of America

CONTENTS

Deathstalkers are one of the most deadly species of scorpion.

CHAPTER ONE

A Fitting Name

The deathstalker scorpion deserves its deadly name. It is often considered to be the most dangerous kind of scorpion in the world. Deathstalker **venom** can kill children and the elderly, and sometimes even healthy adults.

Scorpions are arachnids, a group of eight-legged **invertebrates** that also includes spiders, ticks, and mites. In addition to their eight legs, deathstalkers have two pincers. They also have a long, narrow tail

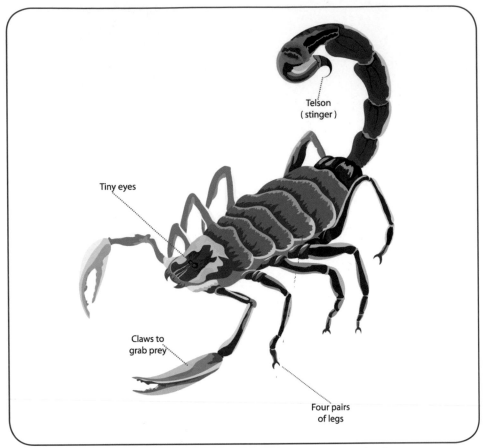

Telson
(stinger)

Tiny eyes

Claws to
grab prey

Four pairs
of legs

All scorpions have a similar body type, with eight legs, pincers, and a stinger.

that ends in a stinger filled with venom. Deathstalkers
are a yellowish-green color, with an **exoskeleton** that
can look almost plastic.

A Hot Habitat

Deathstalker scorpions live in dry desert areas.
Temperatures in their habitat can reach more than
110 degrees Fahrenheit (43 degrees Celsius). During
the scorching heat of the day, they usually rest
underground. They may dig their own burrows, or
take over (or even sometimes share) the burrows of
other animals.

Deathstalker scorpions live in very hot, dry desert regions of the Middle East and North Africa.

Patient Hunting

To avoid the heat, deathstalkers hunt at night. Deathstalkers rely on camouflage to remain unseen as they wait for their prey to come near them. They

A deathstalker in captivity devours a cricket. Beside it is its exoskeleton, or the outer shell scorpions shed when they grow.

don't actively chase their food. When a cricket, centipede, spider, or smaller scorpion comes near, the deathstalker will grab it with its pincers. The pincers look dangerous, but they aren't very strong. If the prey fights back, the deathstalker instantly stings, injecting deadly venom.

Predator or Prey?

Despite being so toxic, the deathstalker scorpion often becomes a meal itself. Larger deathstakers will eat smaller ones. Big centipedes and other species of scorpions also eat deathstalkers. It is a battle of speed against speed, venom against venom. Sometimes the deathstalker loses. Bats also eat a lot of deathstalker scorpions. They seem to be immune to the venom. Bats will start to eat a deathstalker while being stung. They will even eat the venom sac.

If a deathstalker scorpion isn't eaten by something, it will probably live about five years in the wild. Some can live longer in captivity.

Scorplings

When deathstalkers are going to mate, they do an elaborate ritual. The male will circle the female, and then grab her pincers in his own. They will then dance together for several minutes.

For deathstalkers, and many other scorpions, the babies develop inside the mother's body. They are then born alive. The babies—called **scorplings**— look like tiny versions of the adults. There can be more than eighty scorplings in a litter. They grow through about seven instars, or stages. In each instar, they molt. This means they shed their hard exoskeleton. They are in danger until the new

Mother deathstalkers, similar to this scorpion, carry their babies on their backs until the scorplings are big enough to take care of themselves.

exoskeleton hardens. Mother scorpions often carry their scorplings on their backs, keeping them safe. Scorplings stay with their mothers until they molt at least one time.

Deathstalker Scorpion Quick Facts

Name: The deathstalker scorpion's scientific name is *Leiurus quinquestriatus*. It is also called the Israeli yellow scorpion, the Palestine yellow scorpion, the Naqab Desert scorpion, and the Omdurman scorpion. Its common name, deathstalker, comes from its highly venomous sting. Its Latin name means "five-striped smooth tail."

Range: Deathstalkers live in dry scrub and desert areas in North Africa and the Middle East.

Size: Males can reach 3 inches (7.5 centimeters), while females can reach 4 inches (10 cm).

Subspecies: There are two subspecies of deathstalkers. *Leiurus quinquestriatus quinquestriatus* lives in North Africa, and *Leiurus quinquestriatus hebraeus* lives in the Middle East.

Fun Fact: Deathstalkers have six eyes, but they still have very bad vision. They mostly perceive their world through touch and vibration.

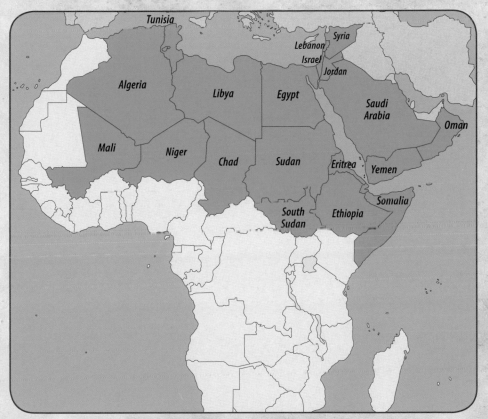

Deathstalkers live in the Middle Eastern and North African countries colored in green.

Animals like this deadly cobra are venomous.

Deadly Sting

People often use the word "poison" to describe any harmful substance. In fact, though, there are distinctions between the terms "poisonous," "toxic," and "venomous."

A **toxin** is a harmful substance that is made by animals, plants, or other organisms. A toxic substance is considered poisonous if it causes harm when it is ingested (eaten) or if it enters the body another way, such as through the skin or lungs. Poison dart frogs, for example, are poisonous because the toxins in their skin cause harm if the frogs are eaten, or if the poison gets in a cut on the skin.

A toxin is called a venom if it is injected into the body by an animal. Some snakes are venomous because they inject venom with fangs like hypodermic needles. Some jellyfish, spiders, and scorpions are also venomous.

A Killer Stinger

The deathstalker scorpion is a venomous creature. It has a stinger on the end of its tail with a bulbous venom sac and a sharp needle for injecting the venom. All scorpions are venomous. However, out of more than a thousand species of scorpions that have been identified, only twenty-five have venom that is strong enough to potentially kill a human.

Venom helps scorpions catch their food. The deathstalker stabs prey with its stinger. The venom is so powerful that the prey will stop struggling within a few seconds.

Self-Defense

Deathstalkers and other scorpions also use their venom for defense. If a larger desert-dwelling animal like a fox or a jackal tries to eat a deathstalker, it may get stung. Like many venomous animals (such

Deathstalker scorpions inject venom with the stinger on the end of their tails.

as rattlesnakes), the deathstalker can **regulate** the amount of venom it injects. If it injects a small amount, the attacker may just be in great pain. If it injects a lot, the attacker may die. Venomous animals will often try to use as little venom as possible to take care of a situation. Venom takes time and energy for the scorpion to produce.

The desert long-eared bat is immune to scorpion venom, and it eats deathstalkers.

The Deadliest Scorpion

Deathstalker scorpions are often considered the most dangerous scorpions on Earth. Even though there are a couple of other scorpion species whose venom is just as strong, deathstalkers are more often found close to where humans live. So they are both extremely toxic and often come into contact with people.

If left untreated, between 1 and 10 percent of all stings will be fatal. The stings are particularly dangerous to children, whose small body size means the poison can spread more quickly and fully through their body. Sick and elderly people are also more likely to die from deathstalker stings.

Pain, Paralysis, and Death

The first symptom of a deathstalker sting is extreme pain. Symptoms can include headache, vomiting, and difficulty breathing. The potentially fatal effects come from a protein in the venom called **chlorotoxin**. This protein interferes with signals that tell muscle cells when to relax and when to contract. When chlorotoxin enters the body, muscles all start to flex. This begins to **paralyze** the body, or make it unable to move. Eventually, someone who is paralyzed may not be able to breathe.

Even though a deathstalker sting isn't always fatal, anyone who is stung should go to the hospital right away. Several kinds of deathstalker scorpion **antivenom** are available. These can reverse the venom's effects. Often, the patient needs many doses to fully recover.

Despite their danger, deathstalkers are sold around the world as pets. The United States, Australia, and some other countries stock deathstalker antivenom in case careless pet owners get stung.

Deathstalker Discovery

The deathstalker scorpion was classified by Christian Gottfried Ehrenberg, a German naturalist who explored Egypt and the

Middle East in the early 1800s. He gave the deathstalker its Latin name. It is unknown if he knew about the scorpion's deadly venom, but it is likely he did. His large collection of Middle Eastern scorpions and spiders is now in the Berlin Natural History Museum.

Explorer and scientist Christian Gottfried Ehrenberg first officially identified the deathstalker scorpion in 1828.

Scientists are careful when extracting scorpion venom.

CHAPTER THREE

Attacking Cancer

Glioma is one of the most common, and most dangerous, types of brain cancer. Chlorotoxin—the main component of deathstalker venom—binds very easily to glioma cells, but not to healthy brain cells. When the chlorotoxin sticks to a cancer cell in the brain it can help doctors in a couple of ways. Where can scientists get this chlorotoxin? They can extract it from the deathstalker scorpion.

A Cancer Cure?

Chlorotoxin is being tested for use in gene therapy. This treatment inserts genes that can act as treatment directly into cancer cells. Sometimes it is hard to tell which cells are cancerous, or to target each individual cell. If doctors have a substance like chlorotoxin that binds to glioma cells, they can use that toxin as a delivery system to get the treatment to the right cells.

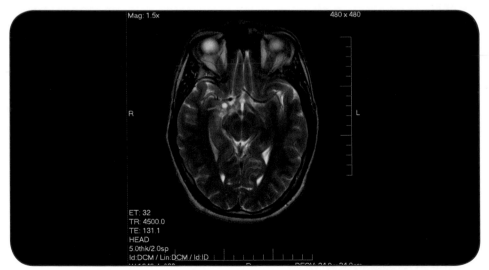

A glioma, such as this one visible in a CT scan, is a deadly kind of brain tumor.

Chlorotoxin's attraction to cancerous glioma cells can also be helpful when used as a marker during surgery. When cutting a tumor out, it is very important that every last trace is removed. If some cells remain, the cancer could return even after surgery. By marking the tumor with a specialized version of chlorotoxin, a surgeon can see which are healthy cells and which are cancerous cells. The cancerous cells "light up" because of a special dye attached to the chlorotoxin.

Deathstalker scorpions also hold a very important place in their environment. Ecologists use deathstalkers and other scorpions to monitor the health of ecosystems. If the area is stable, unpolluted, and undamaged, there should be a healthy number of scorpions. This shows that there are enough prey animals to feed the scorpions. However, if there is environmental damage, one of the first signs of harm

Scorpions glow under ultraviolet light, making them easier for scientists to find at night.

will be a drop in the number of scorpions. When scientists observe that, they know they have to pay special attention to saving or restoring that region.

Deathstalker scorpions live in some of the harshest environments on Earth. Still, as human populations expand, people are living and working nearer to deathstalker territory. The result is that deathstalker habitats are being destroyed. It also means that the dangerous scorpions are coming into contact with people more often. Right now, deathstalker populations worldwide don't appear to be threatened. But scientists monitor deathstalkers and other scorpions to make sure fragile desert ecosystems survive.

Deathstalkers and other scorpions can show the health of an ecosystem.

Toxic Creatures Quiz

1. How does a mother scorpion care for her scorplings?

2. What animal, mentioned in the text, is probably immune to deathstalker stings and often eats them?

3. True or False: Venom is a toxin that causes harm when it is eaten, inhaled, or absorbed through the skin.

4. What kind of cancer tumor does the deathstalker venom chlorotoxin bind to?

Answer Key

1. She carries them on her back until they are big enough to survive alone.

2. Bats (specifically desert long-eared bats).

3. False. Venom is a toxin that causes harm when injected by an animal's fangs or stinger.

4. Glioma.

GLOSSARY

antivenom A substance given to fight the effects of venom from an animal such as a scorpion or a venomous snake.

chlorotoxin The main component of deathstalker venom.

exoskeleton A supportive outer covering for an animal.

glioma The most common and dangerous kind of brain cancer.

invertebrates A group of animals that lack a backbone.

paralyze To make a living animal unable to move.

regulate To adjust or control the amount of something.

scorpling A baby scorpion, which is often carried on its mother's back.

toxin A harmful substance that is made by animals, plants, or other organisms.

venom A toxin made by an animal that is injected from a stinger or fang.

FIND OUT MORE

Books

Pallotta, Jerry. *Tarantula vs. Scorpion*. Who Would Win? New York: Scholastic, 2012.

Singer, Marilyn. *Venom*. Minneapolis, MN: Millbrook Press, 2007.

Websites

ASU School of Life Sciences Ask a Biologist: Venom

https://askabiologist.asu.edu/venom/scorpion_venom

This site has diagrams showing how scorpion venom paralyzes muscle cells.

San Diego Zoo Kids: Scorpions

http://kids.sandiegozoo.org/animals/arthropods/scorpion

This site has key information about scorpions in general.

INDEX

Page numbers in **boldface** are illustrations. Entries in **boldface** are glossary terms.

ABOUT THE
AUTHOR

Laura L. Sullivan is the author of more than forty fiction and nonfiction books for children, including the fantasies *Under the Green Hill* and *Guardian of the Green Hill*. She has written many books for Cavendish Square, including four titles in the Toxic Creatures series.